The First Christmas

There are lots of Early Reader
stories you might enjoy.
Look at the back of the book
or, for a complete list, visit
www.orionbooks.co.uk

The First Christmas

Georgie Adams

Illustrated by
Anna Leplar

Orion
Children's Books

The First Christmas was originally published in 1996
by Orion Children's Books
This edition first published in Great Britain in 2012
by Orion Children's Books
a division of the Orion Publishing Group Ltd
Orion House
5 Upper Saint Martin's Lane
London WC2H 9EA
An Hachette UK Company

1 3 5 7 9 10 8 6 4 2

The Orion Publishing Group's policy is to use papers
that are natural, renewable and recyclable products
and made from wood grown in sustainable forests.
The logging and manufacturing processes are expected
to conform to the environmental regulations
of the country of origin.

A catalogue record for this book is available
from the British Library.

ISBN 978 1 4440 0616 2

Printed and bound in China

www.orionbooks.co.uk

For my father, Felix Legare
G.A.

For my mother
A.C.L.

The story of Christmas is
about a special birthday, which
happened in a place called
Palestine a very long time ago.

It all began when an angel came to see a young woman called Mary. The angel's name was Gabriel and he came to give Mary a message from God.

Mary had heard all about angels but she had never seen one before. When Mary saw Gabriel, she was frightened.

"Don't be frightened," said Gabriel. "God wants you to be the mother of his son.

He will be the most important baby ever born, and you will name him Jesus."

Soon after that, Mary married
a man called Joseph.

Another angel had told Joseph
all about Mary's special baby,
and he promised to love Jesus
as his own son.

At that time, the emperor
of Rome was counting people,
because everyone had to pay
him money.

Everybody had to go back to the town where they were born to be counted. It was very difficult for people who lived far away.

Mary and Joseph lived in
Nazareth, but Joseph had been
born in Bethlehem. So he and
Mary had to make the long
journey to Bethlehem.

Mary rode all the way on a donkey. By the time they got to Bethlehem Mary was very tired. Her baby was coming at any moment!

"We must find somewhere
to rest," said Joseph.

They went straight to an inn
but the innkeeper had to turn
them away.

"Sorry," he said. "No room."

No room! Joseph was really
worried.

They went from house to
house looking for somewhere
to stay. But there were hundreds
of people in Bethlehem and
everywhere was full.

At last, when it was dark, they
found a stable. The kind owner
gave Mary's donkey food
and water.

Mary lay down to rest on a
bed of straw.

And that night, baby Jesus
was born.

Mary gently wrapped her baby
to keep him snug and warm.
Joseph spread soft hay inside
a manger.

Mary and Joseph watched as
the newborn baby slept.

In the hills around Bethlehem,
some shepherds were looking
after their sheep.

It was late at night, but
the shepherds were wide awake.
Wild animals were always on
the look-out for lambs.

Everything was peaceful until
the shepherds saw a bright light.
They covered their eyes, and
wondered what was happening.

Then a voice spoke.
It was an angel.

"Don't be frightened," said the angel. "A king has been born in Bethlehem. The baby is God's son. Go and see him. You will find him in a stable, lying in a manger."

The shepherds could hardly believe their ears. They were amazed.

As soon as the angel had
finished speaking, music filled
the air.

All the angels in heaven
were singing to God! Then
all was still and quiet.

The shepherds looked up at the
stars, but the angels had gone.

"We must hurry to Bethlehem,"
said the shepherds.

First they made sure their
sheep were safe. Then they ran
down the hill and went to
look for the newborn king.

The streets of Bethlehem were quiet as the shepherds looked for the stable.

Suddenly they heard a noise.
It was a baby crying! After that
they found the stable easily.

"Come in," said Mary.

The shepherds went inside
and found Jesus in the manger —
just as the angel had said.

There were three rich wise men, living far away from Bethlehem. These men had spent many years learning about the stars.

One night they saw a new
star. It was brighter than any
they had seen before.

The wise men were sure it
was a sign that a new king had
been born.

So they got on to their camels
and followed the star.

It led them over hills. Across
deserts. Along rivers.

The star guided them all the
way to Bethlehem.

It shone right over the stable
where Jesus lay.

Mary and Joseph welcomed
the three wise men in their
fine clothes.

But as soon as the wise men saw the baby Jesus, they knelt on the dusty floor and worshipped him.

The three wise men gave
Jesus gold, frankincense and
myrrh — three special gifts for
a newborn king.

And that's the story of the very first Christmas long, long ago.

Did you enjoy reading the story of *The First Christmas*? Can you remember the things that happened?

Who gave Mary a message from God?

Who did Mary marry?

What was the emperor doing at that time?

How did Mary travel to Bethlehem?

Where was baby Jesus born?

What did the angel say
to the shepherds?

What did the three wise men think
when they saw the new star?

What special gifts did the wise men
give to the baby Jesus?

The Three Little Princesses

Tan-tan-terrah!

Meet Phoebe, Pruella and Pip.

It's the king's birthday but everything
will go wrong unless the three little
princesses can find the missing
key to the magic clock.

£4.99

978 1 84255 633 7

The Three
Little Pirates

Ahoy there!

Meet Tammy, Trixie and Trig.

The three little pirates must follow the clues
to save the mermaid princess and her friends.

£4.99

978 1 4440 0084 9

The Three Little Witches

Hubble bubble!

Meet Zara, Ziggy and Zoe.

The three little witches are having a party,
but naughty Melissa is out to make trouble!

£4.99

978 1 4440 0080 1

Look out for other Early Reader
stories you might enjoy:

Runaway Duckling

Where Are My Lambs?

Billy The Kid Goes Wild

Barnyard Hullabaloo

Mish Mash Hash

Chicks Just Want to Have Fun

Moo Baa Baa Quack

Meet
the Gang

Yum Yum

Rampage
in Prince's
Garden

Jogger's
Big
Adventure

the Haunted House of Buffin Street

Miaow Miaow Bow Wow

Look at Me